# What Is a Reptile?

by Lola M. Schaefer

chameleon

Consulting Editor: Gail Saunders-Smith, Ph.D.

Consultant: Dwight Lawson, Ph.D.
General Curator, Zoo Atlanta

## Pebble Books

an imprint of Capstone Press
Mankato, Minnesota

Pebble Books are published by Capstone Press
151 Good Counsel Drive, P.O. Box 669, Mankato, Minnesota 56002
http://www.capstone-press.com

2 3 4 5 6 06 05 04 03 02 01

Library of Congress Cataloging-in-Publication Data
Schaefer, Lola M., 1950–
    What is a reptile?/by Lola M. Schaefer.
    p. cm.—(The Animal Kingdom)
    Includes bibliographical references (p. 23) and index.
    ISBN 0-7368-0868-X
    1. Reptiles—Juvenile literature. [1. Reptiles.] I. Title. II. Series.
QL644.2 .S333 2001
597.9—dc21                                                                    00-009673

Summary: Simple text and photographs present kinds of reptiles and their
general characteristics.

# Note to Parents and Teachers

The Animal Kingdom series supports national science standards
related to the diversity of life. This book describes the characteristics
of reptiles and illustrates various kinds of reptiles. The photographs
support early readers in understanding the text. The repetition of
words and phrases helps early readers learn new words. This book
also introduces early readers to subject-specific vocabulary words,
which are defined in the Words to Know section. Early readers may
need assistance to read some words and to use the Table of
Contents, Words to Know, Read More, Internet Sites, and
Index/Word List sections of the book.

# Table of Contents

komodo dragon

caiman

Reptiles are part of
the animal kingdom.
Some reptiles live
on land. Some reptiles
live in water.

Reptiles are cold-blooded.
Their body temperature
is the same as their
surroundings.

alligator

# Reptiles have a skeleton.

hognose snake

Reptiles breathe air
through lungs.

crocodile

# Reptiles have scales.

iguana

Many reptiles
eat other animals.

chameleon

Some reptiles eat plants.

California pond turtle

Some female reptiles give birth to young.

brown snake with young

Most female reptiles lay eggs. Young reptiles hatch from eggs.

loggerhead turtle

# Words to Know

**animal kingdom**—the group that includes all animals

**cold-blooded**—having a body temperature that is the same as the temperature of the surroundings; fish, amphibians, and reptiles are cold-blooded animals.

**female**—an animal that can give birth to young animals or lay eggs; most female reptiles lay eggs, but some give birth to young.

**hatch**—to break out of an egg

**lung**—a body that animals use to breathe

**scales**—small, hard plates that cover the body of a fish or reptile; reptiles have dry scales.

**skeleton**—a framework of bones inside the body

**temperature**—the measure of how hot or how cold something is.

# Read More

**Kalman, Bobbie.** *What Is a Reptile?* The Science of Living Things. New York: Crabtree Publishing, 1999.

**MacLeod, Beatrice.** *Reptiles.* Wonderful World of Animals. Milwaukee: Gareth Stevens, 1997.

**Savage, Stephen.** *Reptiles.* What's the Difference? Austin, Texas: Raintree Steck-Vaughn, 2000.

**Stone, Lynn M.** *What Makes a Reptile?* Animal Kingdom. Vero Beach, Fla.: Rourke, 1997.

# Internet Sites

**Animals of the World**
http://www.kidscom.com/games/animal/animal.html

**Classifying Critters**
http://www.hhmi.org/coolscience/critters/critters.html

**Reptile Printouts**
http://www.zoomschool.com/subjects/reptiles/printouts.shtml

#  Index/Word List

**Word Count: 67**
**Early-Intervention Level: 13**

**Editorial Credits**
Mari C. Schuh, editor; Kia Bielke, cover designer and illustrator; Kimberly Danger, photo researcher

**Photo Credits**
Brandon D. Cole, 20
Craig Brandt, cover (lower right)
Dwight R. Kuhn, cover (lower left), 18
Frederick D. Atwood, 8
Jay Ireland & Georgienne E. Bradley, 16
Joe McDonald/Bruce Coleman Inc., 4 (bottom)
Joe McDonald/McDonald Wildlife Photography, cover (upper right), 12, 14
PhotoDisc, Inc., 1, 6
Ronald Cantor, 10
Visuals Unlimited/Charles W. McRae, cover (upper left); Ken Lucas, 4 (top)